THE LAYMAN'S HANDBOOK
OF
INTERIOR DESIGN

The Layman's
Handbook
of
Interior Design

Ellen Angell, A. I. D.

An Exposition-Banner Book

EXPOSITION PRESS   **NEW YORK**

EXPOSITION PRESS INC.

50 Jericho Turnpike   Jericho, New York 11753

FIRST EDITION

LIBRARY OF CONGRESS CATALOG CARD NUMBER: 75-171703

0-682-47363-4

To Muggs and Loren, with love

CONTENTS

PREFACE

I HAVE BEEN THINKING about such a book as this for years, and only through the urging of friends and clients have I considered putting it on paper.

As the profession of interior design has grown, there has been much discussion of whether to hire an interior designer or to do it yourself. As each year has passed, educational standards have been raised, and the fields have become more specialized.

Mr. and Mrs. Pace Setter have seen the fallacies of costly mistakes through lack of design knowledge when they attempted to do it themselves. This same Mr. and Mrs. Pace Setter, however, are doers and need projects to keep them busy as well as to fill the empty corners of their dwelling; so I am not suggesting that they hire someone to do everything.

After twenty-two years in this profession, I am still appalled at the examples of bad taste prevalent in this country, whether it be bad architecture or interior design. So many well-designed homes have been adulterated through poor remodeling, both on the exterior and interior. Fine furniture, refinished in a color wrong for the period for which it was designed, with hardware styles of yet another era, tends to debase the home. My constant cry is that any design that was originally a good design is still a good design if properly used.

We are fast destroying our heritage simply because we do not want to go to reference books, whether on our bookshelf or at the public library, to authenticate our projects. Of course, we don't live in museums today. We live in homes with all the conveniences of the modern age, but there is no reason we can't have good design and build homes which will house those precious pieces of wood which are no longer available and which will become more and more precious as the years go on. On the proper maintenance of these furnishings you cannot be excused because of ignorance. Carefully read Chapter VI on care of your fine furniture and maintenance of fabrics in your home.

How urgently I feel the need for proper restoration in our country! All too few in our land are concerned about preserving the old, as modern buildings replace miles upon miles of Americana. I know in my heart that you, the individual, could do more about it if only you would—a flower box on your patio or attached to your window; a tree for the park; a helping hand to the city fathers for a garden and its maintenance at the entrance to your town.

Beauty inside or outside your home is contagious. The honest effort of acting through group participation is a thing of the past for too many. You have to give to receive, and anything not shared is soon lost.

You owe it to your family, to your friends, and to the visitors who come to your door, to create beauty in any way that you can. Of course, you have talent in your own way as I do in mine. Take fifteen minutes a day to sit quietly and think. Let your mind be passive, and you will develop an awareness that will probably surprise even you. Through this awareness, ideas will occur to you to develop and beautify the world around you. Statistics tells us that each individual directly influences ten people. Think how far-reaching a beautification program could be. I know many are involved in such organizations as service clubs, but my question is, how involved? Do you go home and put into practice what you have learned? It is my hope that this book will help you in some measure to do so.

I would be remiss if, at this time, I did not thank those who contributed to the physical development of this book: Sue Payne and Phyllis Angell for the secretarial work; Richard Angell, my illustrator; and my many friends and clients who have each contributed a part to make a whole. I am especially blessed to have had parents who encouraged this development in the years past. All will recognize themselves as they read. With each life we touch we gain something, and to each and everyone of these people I am grateful.

THE LAYMAN'S HANDBOOK
OF
INTERIOR DESIGN

I

BUILDING A HOME

THE ESSENTIALS OF BUILDING a new home, or even remodeling an old one, are basically the same. You need a good interior designer, an architect, and a builder. Too many people have taken short cuts. Some have realized it immediately; others at a later period through cultural growth.

Now this is not an easy task, but it is better to put forth the effort in the beginning than to suffer the frustration later.

There are tens of thousands of people who will tell you that at least one, and probably two people, can be eliminated from this trio. After all, the builder has built many durable homes and will do the same for you, or the architect will carry out the decorating schemes for you because he has studied design, or the interior designer will work with the builder and take care of the details for you. Without all three, you could very well lose much money, much time, and all of your coordinated esthetic effects.

Building a home should be fun, but without all three responsible people on the job helping with decisions, it can be utter hell. Do not take my word for it—ask the person who has built one each way. You may go to the east, west, north or south, and the answers will be the same.

In selecting your architect, you must observe his work and evaluate whether or not it has the "look" you want. Architects, of course, are versatile, but usually do one type of architecture better than others. After telling your architect the "musts" you expect in the house and the maximum amount of money to be spent on the structure, he should explain the way he works and what his fees are. If he does not, then ask before you leave your first meeting with him. His figures are your second expense, the first being the property you have purchased.

Next, if you do not already have an interior designer, start your search. Follow the same procedure as in the selection of the architect. Have a talk with her (or him) and discuss the basic ideas you have put forth to the architect. Then discuss the fees and services, and plan your next appointment when the preliminary floor plans are ready.

At the preliminary-plan conference with your architect, he should explain these plans and make recommendations for the materials that will go into the structure. Ask him for a first and second choice in materials so that you can discuss and consider the finished effect your home will have.

Never lose sight of the fact that it is *your* home, not the architect's or the interior designer's, so you must carefully consider the ideas they present to you.

The preliminary-plan visit with your interior designer is filled with discussion on what the basic structure is and how the home furnishings will be placed on the floor plan. It does not cost a penny to move doors and windows and cabinets at this point so do it now, not later after the work has begun.

During this visit you need to discuss lighting fixtures, hardware, carpet, and plumbing-fixture allowances, so that you will have amply allowed for them in your specifications. This is true especially if you are financing your home with a loan. Most often if an architect or a contractor wants to keep the price down, he will give you unrealistic figures for these items in your specifications.

Remember that only what the specifications say is what the builder is legally bound to give you. Some homes have a full book of specifications, others are but a single sheet. You can be assured that the single-sheet owners are in trouble from the day construction begins. Be sure there is a definite date for completion, otherwise construction could go on forever if the builder is working on other jobs at the same time.

When the blueprints are completed, the task of getting bids begins. Submit your plans only to those builders whose work you have examined. A grave error can be avoided in assuming the taste of another individual meets your standards of excellence. "They say" is fatal. "They," the people recommending a builder, may not care if the woodwork meets at the corners, to say nothing of how the plumbing works. Of course, this is exaggerated to a certain extent, but not as much as you may think. This contractor is the builder, not the designer of the esthetic aspect of your home, and he must function well in this capacity. There is only trouble when the owner questions him on matters of design, for he is often a man who is flattered by such questions and therefore gives an opinion; regardless of its value. I do not want to underestimate the builder, but you do not ask me, the interior designer, how to build a wall. My only point is that many times, the new owner-to-be makes the mistake of discussing each detail with everyone rather than with the proper person to whom this particular problem belongs. You do not go to the dentist for an eye test!

We build only a few homes in our lifetime—possibly only one, and we tend to confuse ourselves by running around in circles asking questions of the wrong people. Approach these problems step by step and they fall into place beautifully.

After the bid is let, plan and select the basic furnishings, the lighting fixtures, plumbing fixtures, hardware, paints, hard floors, and tiles in the first few weeks so they can be ordered. The builder will probably not give you twenty-four hours' notice when he needs them, and if you plan this far ahead they will be available when needed.

You must know at the very beginning, before the bid is

let, what the electrical allowance covers. Does it include all the lighting fixtures, interior and exterior? Does it include the recessed lights? Does it include the cost of installation? Is the wiring bid specified separately?

Does the plumbing bid cover all fixtures? Are the fancy faucets you probably will want included? Does the hardware allowance mean the hinges as well as the knobs and pulls? Does it include the nails in the walls? The thresholds for the doors? The towel racks, soap dishes, toilet-paper holders and toothbrush holders for the house?

If you are using ceramic tile in baths and quarry or Mexican tile on some floors or brick floors or terrazzo, does the bid cover the cleaning and three coats of finish on them (sealer and wax)? If you have wood parquet floors, does the bid include, sanding, staining, finishing, and waxing?

Does the bid include a dirt-free home with windows and fixtures sparkling the day you sign the papers? It is not possible? *It is possible,* and should be part of the agreement before the bid is let. In other words, these are important in your specifications. Spell out everything. Do not listen to anyone who says, "Oh, they always do that." Put it in writing, and you know it will be done.

When planning with your interior designer for this new home, all of your present possessions should be considered, and as many as possible should be used. These furnishings represent you, and in most instances have an intrinsic value. I am not suggesting you use a poorly designed piece that was never worth keeping, but it is a mistake not to use your possessions which have value and are worth keeping. As you know the total store-bought look is not home.

The coordination of floor textures, wall textures (such as wallpapers and wall coverings), ceramic tiles, kitchen appliances, and carpeting must be considered as a whole, not each room individually.

Usually you can tell the do-it-yourself home-economics-major type who knows good things and tries to put all she knows on display under one roof, with dozens of wall and floor changes visible at a glance. This is the time when money is a real deterrent to good design. Simplicity is the key, and it is a large key to turn. Think of all the people you know who wear too many accessories with a patterned ensemble, both men and women. The same applies to the overall appearance of a home. Let your eye sweep over it, and see if your thinking and planning have created a free-flowing ensemble.

In initially planning a home, there are some basic things to consider. Start with the front door, which should be attractive, clean, and of an interesting color. This is what the stranger or friend sees while waiting to be let in. A most important first impression is long-lasting. Have your designer look for some old lamps or lanterns and an interesting door knocker to enrich first impression. Next the entry hall—if possible do have one. The more spacious the entry hall (even in a tiny house) the more spacious the house will seem. Again, keep that first impression in mind. You must put one or two or more of your finer pieces where they will be seen at the first glance. My advice has always been to do the entry well, even if the rest of the home suffers to a certain degree. This is the preview of what is in the rest of the home. Make it right!

Your living room or parlor should be furnished with items that will fulfill the function the room will have. Is it to be a room for entertaining couples with conversation, couples with bridge, ladies for teas, or ladies for meetings? This will determine the seating plan. Will it be used for daytime functions or nightime functions? Each particular occasion requires a different emphasis. Do not overlook the proper lighting in each instance. It is, of course, possible to incorporate the two. This requires more forethought and planning. Today it is certainly possible to be both elegant and practical. Simple elegance is a challenge that needs much consideration.

The dining room is regaining popularity, even in smaller

homes. People who have always had them are once more beginning to use them, but most often, in a different way. The food is being wheeled in from the kitchen and either served buffet style or family style, depending on the occasion. This room should always be ready for meals. If it is ready to function, you will use it.

The kitchen has been glamorized to the point that everyone is now aware of the latest design in appliances and short-cuts in cooking. Probably the one thing that has always been neglected in this area is where Mrs. Homemaker will keep her own cooking utensils. If she would live in the kitchen mentally at the preliminary-planning stage, it could be much more efficient when she actually moves in. It is simple to build drawers to fit pots, pans, and lids, cabinet areas to house the cannisters and spices and the counter tops properly coordinated for mixing pastries and cakes, and for preparing salads and vegetables. The pantry shelves can be narrow and close together so there is no need for stacking. Reserve stock can be seen at a glance. When we have to expend the effort we rarely do the chore at hand. So make it easy on yourself.

Do not eat in the kitchen. Make a small nook out of the way of the dirty pots and pans in a colorful area with long windows where the outdoors can be seen. If there are only two feet of ground, with a little bamboo fence, and you cannot grow flowers, put out a bird feeder. Even the city birds will find you. And if you have not learned by now, long windows add space to any room.

The next room to tackle is the family room, study, or library. I personally object to the term "den" since people, not animals will inhabit it. The first consideration is the function of this area: is it a study area, a reading room, or a television-viewing room? When this function is determined, then the furnishings can be considered. Study and reading rooms require special consideration for areas that will accommodate desk, writing tables, comfortable chairs, and good light (daylight and artificial) to save the eyes. If the television viewing is done in the daytime, there must be draperies to cut out the daylight and soft light provided for night viewing. The seating must be planned for the number of people who will normally view the programs. Again it is poor planning not to have an area ready for use at all times. If a hostess must tear up her room to entertain, then all is lost. She will be nervous and never settle down, and the guests will be sorry they came.

The other wing of the home is the resting wing and should be designed from start to finish to accommodate the needs of each individual. Bedrooms should be arranged so that the beds are placed away from view of the doorway if possible. There should be ample closets for the storage of hats, handbags, shoes, coats, suits, dresses, and apparel. If you sleep in the daytime, you will need heavy draperies to shut out the light. If you read in your bedroom, an easy chair and lamp are necessary. If you read in bed, special considerations must be given to nightstand lamps.

Dressing areas and baths have taken on a look of elegance in recent years, with many interesting hard surfaces available for counters. Be sure to consider the finished effect of your counter in relation to your lavatory and how easily it will clean before you make your final decision. Pretest the synthetics. If, for instance, you want a synthetic lavatory bowl, take the sample and let a drippy faucet run over it for a week, and see if it pits or changes color or texture. The water of each area has a different mineral content and will affect the porous surfaces differently as they will metals used in decorative faucets and plungers. By pretesting, you know personally what it will do. It is also worthwhile to test your cleansers on these materials so you can see what you can and can't do to your own bathroom.

Storage is very important. Plan those extra closets for everything: out-of-season clothes, camera equipment, records (both files and stereo), books, luggage, silver and china, camping equipment, sports equipments, and the like. Plan now, not after you move in.

If you need a hobby room, sewing room or utility room, consider an area that will be convenient. And do so now. At least build the floor, outside walls, and roof for later completion. It is much cheaper to do it now than to add the whole room later.

Avoid having a garage at the front of the house, loaded with junk and with the doors always open. There is no excuse for such an eyesore. Plan ample storage spaces with doors, and finish the interior of your garage even down to the paint job. If you cannot afford to finish it, at least give everything a coat of charcoal paint.

II

COLOR

COLOR IS PROBABLY THE MOST effective means of expressing your own individuality in the home. Since we are greatly affected by color this should be given considerable thought.

Think of your favorite color, the one you most enjoy around you. It may be too hot a color to be used throughout your room, but it could be used liberally if properly balanced with its complement. Look at any color wheel that is available to you. You will find the colors opposite are complementary, and adjoining colors make a pleasant scheme. Naturally you do not use them all in the same intensity. Some are soft and others are bold and strong.

At this point in your thinking you need to learn a little about yourself and your need for certain colors.

By now you have learned the colors most pleasant for you. Are you a blue person? A green person? A red person? Let's take a look at you.

Red—a leadership color. Most of our famous leaders of the past and present are strongly attracted to this color. This is the color of your blood, a vital color. Many of nature's flowers are a beautiful, clear red as is healthy blood. Red is vital, vibrant, and exhilarating. If you need renewed energy look at something red while you drink a glass of water, and you will be refreshed after fifteen minutes.

This is why we use small amounts of it in our most lived-in areas. If it is a very active area then use larger quantities. This color is pulsating and must be used carefully around people with high blood pressure and nervous disorders. The complement to red is green.

Orange—a health color. It is a combination of red and yellow. The Orientals consider this a very fine color and identify it with their religions. To be enjoyed, this color must be clear in tone, as in fruit, not a muddy tone. People who need stimulation will find this an excellent color. It is less vibrant than red and more suitable for a person with an overactive heart or a lung condition. The complement to orange is blue.

Yellow—a knowledge color. I always like to say, "Yellow denotes genius." It represents knowledge, and when a person whose favorite color is yellow reads of something new, he will look up information about it in order to have a speaking acquaintance of it. Yellow also represents a deep and abiding faith within the individual. This person is basically very good and wants to do the right thing. The complement to yellow is purple.

Green—a growing color. New growth is green and represents growing; therefore, you could also call it a health color. People whose favorite color is green want large windows in their homes, with plants inside as well as outside. They will have some kind of garden whether it be flowers, plants, or a kitchen garden. They will like picnics, and their home will be easy to care for so they will have time for such outings. The complement to green is red.

Blue—a teaching color. This is the color of our sky most of the time. Like green-fanciers, blue people will want spaciousness and large window areas in their home. They will want to see the patch of blue available to them from their windows, and this feeling gives them the space they may lack within their four walls. Blue people make good instructors; this includes executives and teachers. It is a color that represents faith in any project. A proficient instructor believes deeply in his field. The deeper the blue the individual prefers, the more mature he is. The complement to blue is orange.

Turquoise—the combination of blue and green. If the color inclines more toward one than the other, select the same hue in your complement, i.e., a green turquoise takes a redder orange than a blue turquoise.

Indigo or Purple—a wisdom color. It is the color of royalty. Someone who likes excessive amounts of purple is usually a depressed person or one who has suffered a tragedy in his life. This color is heavy and oppressive in large quantities. Use it sparingly in your home and add yellow, its complement.

Designers today have facilitated the selection of a design and the use of its colors. If only we will carry out what they say about design. Notice the ratio of one color to the overall design, and repeat it in your room in the same ratio. If the design is basically red, naturally you would have more of its complement, green, in a much softer intensity than in the case of a red room, which would in time become rather oppressive.

A room's color intensity is best determined by you. If you spend many hours a day in a given room, make it much softer and more subtle; if only a few hours for fun, make it bright and intense. Never lose sight of the room's function. Make the color of a bedroom quiet and recessive. The library, or combination bedroom-study should not be done in distracting colors. A fun room however, should be full of intense, lively color. And so it goes throughout the house.

If planning a new home, key the whole house to three colors, e.g., green, red, and yellow with two colors such as brown and white, used more sparingly. All the walls, carpeting, or hard floors could be green, but this is not my idea of an attractive home; it is just playing it safe. Let this be your rule of thumb: all areas opening into each other that can be partially viewed simultaneously should be in single color. This lends a feeling of spaciousness to the house. Since your eye stops at each color change, avoid the choppy effect of too many colors in any given area.

Complementaries intensify their colors, and so for variety's sake use them wherever accents are needed.

How do I know which blue goes with which orange and which green goes with which red? Think about this carefully, and observe that each color has a certain amount of yellow (sunlight) in it—simply put the same amount of sunlight in each color whether it is very strong and or very pastel. It works.

Today when everyone is becoming a number, it is difficult to be an individual. But no two of us have the same eyes, hair, skin texture, and general coloring, except in the case of a few identical twins. For this reason, our color needs are different. Dare to be different; dare to use color in your home. Designers are color-key conscious, and to a great extent we have been unconscious of their influence on us.

Think of the rust and browns of the twenties, the rose and blues of the thirties, the red, green, and chartreuse of the forties, the turquoise and corals of the fifties, and the golds and muddy greens of the sixties. The fabrics, furniture, linens, kitchenware, and even the garbage pails are color-keyed. So unless you want to custom-dye everything for your home, take the current trends and availability of colors into consideration.

There are often circumstances that control the availability of a color, such as the rich blue dye unavailable in the 1950's because all cobalt was being used for cancer treatment and research; at that time all good, rich blues were basically cobalt. We in the design field had to await the development of a good synthetic blue dye before using it once again in our schemes.

Color is used in industry and in merchandising. Why do you think the red and yellow boxes of washing powder sell so much faster than the blue and green boxes? The former of course come out to meet you, and the latter recede. Color is used to making working conditions more pleasant so that you, the employee, can be more productive. Color is a way of life whether you are aware of it or not.

This is a time for awareness. Look at a leaf with its varying hues of green, and a plant's delicately shaded bloom. Learn from nature that the blooms come and go in small amounts of bright color. Our sky is only red at sunset, not all day long. Of course we can live with green and brown, blue and gray—nature's large quantities of color—for an extended time.

Make a red, orange, or bright yellow room if you wish, but be sure (like the flower in the garden) that it's a small area not constantly lived in, and surround it with more restful colors in adjoining areas.

A child's room should be soft in color until he reaches the age of six. Show me a child's room in hot, bright colors, and I'll show you an overly active and probably very nervous little girl or boy.

To be different is a real challenge because we fear what our friends, family, and visitors will say. But in reality, if the colors in our homes suit us individually, there can be no criticism on that score.

You, your family, and your guests are delightfully interesting individuals, so why not be different and set trends which provide a background for you to be king or queen of your domain? Be seen at your best as soon as your door is opened.

III

CARPETS AND RUGS

THE MOST UNRELIABLE MARKET today is in rugs and carpets. These products are misrepresented to the public to such an extent that I am amazed at the various stories I hear.

For instance, carpet nylon and nylon carpet are two different things. Carpet nylon is a tough, high-denier type of fiber that cleans easily, recovers quickly; and no dirt or stain, except mustard and orange juice, ever penetrate the fiber. This fiber is usually a long stable fiber, not short sluffings which ball up when walked on. Nylon carpet can be any nylon, such as sweater or hosiery fibers or soft fibers mixed with sluffings from the good nylon that causes the pilling you see on cheap carpets. This quality of fiber absorbs dirt, packs when walked on, and will not clean. Buyers of nylon carpet give all nylon a bad name. Either they do not want their friends to know they purchased a cheap carpet, or the salesman misrepresented the fiber to them when they purchased it.

My choice after carpet nylon is a comparatively new polyester fiber. The wear tests have shown excellent results and I can confidently recommend this fiber. But how the manufacturers will treat it remains to be seen. So many marvelous synthetic fibers have been produced by chemical companies, only to have them misused by carpet manufacturers, who sometimes make a practice of cutting them when they should not be. This makes the fiber virtually unusable, but the reliable fiber sources have spent thousands of dollars on advertising, and the carpet manufacturers often cash in on adulterated fiber. Someday, I hope, we will be told what we are buying and what it will do. The polyester should be cared for as if it were carpet nylon.

My third choice for carpeting is wool. It would be my first if it could be obtained at a reasonable price. There are inexpensive wools on the market today, but anything less than $30.00 a square yard is too soft to be used. Synthetics are much less expensive and more durable than wool. Remember that wool now costs three times what it did ten years ago, so be sure your sense of values are updated when you make the statement I hear so often, "Why, my wool only cost $10.00 a square yard when I had it laid ten years ago, and it is still good!"

Domestic wool is too soft. Think of your soft wool skirt or slacks that became rump-sprung and dingy before the season is out. It takes a hard wool from an animal living in an extremely cold climate to grow a tough, durable fiber. In the United States, there are limited seasons; thus, no prolonged cold seasons are available to wool growers. I use as an example Oriental rugs, old and new. They are tough as nails and most lasting.

Several years ago I worked a fire claim, and the area rugs had been purchased from a major carpet company still greatly respected in the industry. These wool rugs were thirty years old and badly damaged by the fire. I wrote the manufacturers regarding the availability, enclosing a sample. Their reply was startling to say the least. They said that the carpeting was no longer available because of the high cost of the fiber. At the time of purchase it was approximately $32.00 a square yard, and if manufactured today, it would cost at least $72.00 a square yard for a similar quality.

Do not misunderstand my opinion on the use of wool. If you can afford it, use it. It is still the finest carpeting, providing it is a durable quality. The care of good wool is simple. The only caution is this: *never* use hot water as part of the cleaning process. It removes oil from the fiber and makes it dry and lifeless.

What about acrilan carpeting? In my opinion it is over-rated, overadvertised, and only the manufacturers benefit from its sale. It does eventually pack down and form traffic areas, and I see no reason to use it as long as better fibers are similarly or lower priced.

"Read the labels" is my watchword. Take a swatch of carpeting home and put everything on it that you could possibly drop on it. Then clean it. This will tell you whether or not it is the carpeting for you. But do not close your eyes to the way it cleans; even a glass of water sometimes changes the texture of a carpet. Yes, just plain water.

I always remember the client who was a builder and planned to live a few months in a new home he was building and then sell it. Naturally he wanted to create the maximum effect with as little expense as possible. I insisted on decent carpeting with quality padding, despite his reservations about the cost. He made his decision only after several days, because he felt I was being unreasonable with his money. When it came to the purchase, he remarked that I had never advised him incorrectly, and so he had to rely on my choice.

We installed the carpeting, and Mr. and Mrs. Builder moved in. One day Mrs. Builder was late for an appointment, turned on the diswasher, and sped away. When she returned several hours later, the house was flooded because the dishwasher had not turned off. The carpeting and padding were taken up, dried, and relaid. To this day, Mr. Builder is a believer. We saved them the expense of replacing this carpeting. The moral of the story is: you get exactly what you pay for.

So many say, "Oh, I only want the carpeting to last two or three years, so let's not put a lot of money in it." It seems impossible for this budget-minded individual to realize that carpeting is not going to look lovely for three years and then suddenly fall apart. It is going to start looking badly in four or five months and continue to grow worse.

Many people spend more per square inch on their bath towels than they do on carpeting which gets constant wear. This kind of thinking on the part of the homemaker is difficult to understand.

When planning a new home, it is wise to plan the room sizes so that the carpet widths fit. For instance, a room 14′6″ will lay with 15-foot carpeting and a 11′6″ room will lay with 12-foot carpeting. This kind of planning gives you fewer seams and means a neater job.

When we lay new carpeting in older homes, we remove the shoe mould and place the tack strip next to the woodwork, thus making a much neater installation. If the shoe mould is removed, you should do the touch-up painting before the carpet installation.

Many people are surprised when our carpet layers leave, and the door are propped up against the walls waiting to be shortened. Of course, it stands to reason that if the doors were close to the floor without carpeting, then the one inch or so of carpeting would naturally affect them. So plan for a carpenter when you contract for the carpeting to be installed. This sometimes necessitates some touch-up painting on the doors.

Many of my clients call me frantically after the carpeting is installed with the complaint that all of the new carpeting is going into the vacuum cleaner. This is the sluffings or cut fibers which sifted down into the pile during production. This happens on the cut pile carpets where the company has clipped and reclipped to get the pile height even.

Any new carpeting should be vacuumed daily the first month so that this loose pile can be removed. Many carpet problems have been solved by the use of a good upright vacuum cleaner with a real pulling power. I know the tank-type cleaners are a necessity for upholstery, draperies, cornices, mattresses, etc.; but the upright is a must for carpeting. The tank type is not satisfactory where a pile carpeting is the problem.

When it comes to area rugs, the age-old problem of rug size is always controversial. My general rule is this: in a small room, the size of the rug is the size of the room. You must plan to get the most from your space, so a rug extending three inches up to twelve to eighteen inches from the wall is best. In a large space where you want to designate the conversation area, place grouping in the room and put all the furniture either touching or upon the rug. This rug will only cover a portion of the complete room area, perhaps half of a room or less.

The area rug is an accent in a large room and must relate to the furnishings and hard floor, but should put some "snap" into the area. Sometimes these rugs are used for purposes other than accents. If they are only for warmth, they should blend with the hard floor as closely as possible and disappear.

Oriental rugs are being purchased for accents and because of demand, I would like to interject a word of caution here. You get exactly what you pay for. Oriental rug buying is an art, and there are many dishonest sellers of Oriental rugs today. You, the innocent purchaser, are their prime target. You want something for nothing, a bargain, and they know more about these rugs than you could ever begin to learn, so why do you think you are going to take one away from them? Please rely on a reputable, well-recommended dealer who has been in business a long time and pay his price. You will be well rewarded for the money and effort spent on this well-shopped purchase.

IV

DRAPERIES AND FABRICS

IT IS BECOMING INCREASINGLY more difficult to get anything custom-made. Fortunately, there are men and women still available who do beautiful work—sewing and upholstering. Most of our draperies and upholstering require handwork and tailoring, which is an art that takes years to master. Hems form a considerable percentage of draperies, and I have never seen a machine blind-stitch a hem that I approved of in clothing, draperies, bedspreads, or valances.

These items, like a well-tailored suit, are easily recognized when they come from the loving hands of the do-it-yourself amateur.

Many fabrics are unfit for hanging at windows, using on beds, or covering furniture. So you must rely on an experienced interior designer who has studied fibers. I sometimes astound students when I inform them that they must take chemistry in their interior-design courses. But with our synthetics today, you certainly need to know how the fibers are produced, what they are made to do, and what they will not do. An excellent fiber, when used for a purpose for which it is not made, will fail. The erroneous conclusion is that the fiber is worthless.

When do I use a sheer printed or plain, at my windows? When do I use a lined drapery, printed or plain? When do I use both? Are cornices and valances in? Will a custom-made bedspread cost $200 or more? Why are drapery rods so expensive?

All these items for the home are made to last from five

to fifteen years with proper care. You can abuse an item in your home within five minutes after delivery, or you can carefully enjoy it to the fullest extent of its life and get your money's worth. Know what you are buying, how it is to be maintained, and you will enjoy owning custom-made things.

Aesthetics enter into custom-made items, and there is such a fine line between good taste and bastard imitations. The untrained do-it-yourselfer really shows his limited knowledge at this point. Also, persons who are self-trained do not even realize what wrongs they are committing in the design world. Of course, there are geniuses who are born with this talent, and I am the first to recognize them. The genius clause in the A.I.D. rules for membership was dropped after three years because geniuses were almost nonexistent.

If the history of a particular era of good design is studied, good contemporized alterations can be made, and you will then have a modernized version of an age-old, time-tested style of design.

Many windows are overdraped because the decorator wants to sell the client as much as the budget will bear. An interior designer will drape the windows with only enough to satisfy the requirements of the family and the total design of the room.

Traverse draperies can be lined or unlined, depending on the privacy required. For instance, you do not want white translucent draperies in a bedroom on the east side of the house if the client needs a dark room in which to sleep. If you are on the street side you will need sheers for privacy in any room of your home.

Valances, cornices, or festoons and cascades can be alternatives if ornamental rods are not used and the plain traverse rods displease you. Personally I prefer the plain rods, painted to match the walls with their uncluttered look.

If you want to accent a window, by all means use a patterned drapery, but be very sure that the rectangular or square shape that this creates is the shape your room requires. Many times you really need the drapery that disappears, that is, one that matches the wall, because you have a focal point in front of the draperies that needs only a background. This, of course, the interior designer will recognize immediately.

As to custom-made bedspreads, these are expensive, but well worth the money if you can afford it. "If you can afford it" is a very big factor in many of our lives, but so often we will do the inexpensive thing, which is false economy. Occasionally I hear the phrase, "Oh, I don't want it to last forever, so I'll spend very little on it." I just nod and do what they want if they will not listen to the economy argument, and within the year begins the criticism about the way it is beginning to look. Then comes a pet phrase with me, "You got exactly what you paid for!" I do not believe we will ever eliminate the desire people have to get something for nothing.

Probably the worst mistake that can be made in estimating draperies is to make them insufficiently full. A skimpy drapery is not worth hanging. Unless you have at least a five-inch fullness in your pleats and a three-and-one-half-inch space between the pleats, you have nothing, and with sheerer fabrics you need more. If you cannot afford a fabric with this fullness, search for one that will give you the effect of fullness with less fabric. I always shudder when I hear, "This is the only fabric that will do." There are always substitutes, but they must be searched out. Both client and designer must be flexible in reselection. Of course the fabric will not be the same in price, but with a little flexibility a suitable substitute can be found.

As to the upholstery fabrics and workmanship you can find any and all kinds, prices, and craftsmanship. But the discerning eye can tell the difference from across the room, and the individual with little aesthetic training can certainly realize upon sitting in a chair, for example, the kind of craftsmanship that went into its construction.

My old statement still stands: you get exactly what you pay for.

Look for the comfort of sitting, the cushion that holds its shape, the welt cords that remain smooth and not wavy, the neatness of the tailoring at the corners, the flatness of the skirt, the cord trim or nail trim completed to perfection. All this is to no avail if the fabric is not tough. By the word "tough," I do not means it has to be rough and ugly. It can be a silk damask, a velvet, a brocade, or any other good fabric, but it must be flexible so it will stretch onto the furniture properly. Again it is the job of the interior designer to determine what the chair will be used for and the kind of fabric it requires. Many times I have found it hard to tell the difference from across the room, or from even closer up, between a fine cotton damask and some silk damasks. Of course, the cotton will outwear most silks, but the dyes are much more effective on the silk.

Life is full of compromise, and one of these could be a decision between durability and a particular color that can only be realized in silk. The flexibility of your choice will depend upon you, the client, and your designer.

We are using more and more man-made fibers for inner construction in our upholstery today simply because of availability. Since we have discovered the allergies to down and feathers, dacron fillings are a real blessing and testing has proven that they last longer. All of these factors must be considered in the purchase of new furniture or the reconstruction of a client's own.

Recently a client asked, "Am I wrong in not wanting to antique my own furniture?" My answer to her was, "Of course not." Her discerning eye knew the difference, and she preferred a professional touch. My complaint is against those who so often settle for less than the best either because they do not know the difference or do not care.

V

FURNITURE

FROM THE TIME OF THE CAVEMEN, when the only tables and stools were rocks, we have endeavored to beautify our habitat. The aborigines drew crude pictures and signs on their walls to add interest. As the ages passed and we became more skilled as craftsmen, embellishment became more frequent and appeared on more objects.

Even during the Renaissance, each piece of furniture had a definite purpose. Chests were for storage as well as sitting, the beds were draped for warmth more than for ornamentation. The backs of some chairs were high to cut off drafts. The chair seats were of a height that could be used at a table for dining as well as for relaxation. The training of craftsmen was often under the aegis of the Church. Therefore, much ecclesiastical influence can be found in many works of art from this age.

Society became more refined as the years went by, and so did the furnishings. For instance, the Louis periods in France, the Queen Anne and Eighteenth Century periods in England, the Duncan Phyfe and Federal of the United States have great curved beauty and smoothness of design.

In selecting furniture for your home, you must first consider the way it will be used, the amount of time you will give to its maintenance, and the kind of overall look you want to achieve. There are certain colors that go with certain periods of furniture, and even though you are not furnishing a museum, you must consider the colors proper to a given period, since they enhance the beauty of its design.

EARLY AMERICAN MOOD

COLONIAL MOOD

Probably the most popular furnishings in today's homes fall in the following categories: Early American, Colonial, Eighteenth Century, French, French Provincial, Spanish or Mediterranean, and Modern.

Early American can be one of the homiest styles, although I personally will not tolerate very many ruffled shades, which I consider a bit too much! But the charm of this period is its calico look, its samplers, rag rugs, textured fabrics, whitewashed wooden walls, brick floors, lantern lamps, pewter pieces, and black wrought-iron hardware.

On today's market, there is a tendency to make every maple piece with the same finish and the same color tone until it becomes monotonous. It takes much careful selection to give an Early American room the necessary warmth and richness of feeling without getting tasteless.

Close kin to this period are the Colonial rooms that call for early Traditional pieces, most often with the darker brown finishes. These rooms, too, take the samplers, the turkeywork, crewel embroideries and any other type of embroidery, the cotton and linen damasks. Today this furniture is sometimes labeled Early English. Because of the darker woods, the colors need to be rich reds and greens and stronger golds and blues to impart the necessary strength to the furniture itself.

The sideboards, the cupboards, the large rectangular tables, the Windsor chairs in their simpler design, and the library and hall tables are typical of this era. Needlepoint is effective in this type of room on furniture as well as rugs. In our history, the Colonial period was filled with patriotism; therefore, the drums, the eagle, and anything of this sort is always correct. Usually a gun is hung on the wall in a handy place.

From this historical period, we move South to the plantation and the finer pieces of furniture which the people of means were able to bring to this country. This is what has developed today into our Traditional or Eighteenth Century

18TH CENTURY-TRADITIONAL MOOD

FRENCH MOOD

furniture. The colors to be used are the same, the rich dark woods and the rich reds, greens, golds, and blues. All accessories follow the lines of the Colonial except in each instance, they are more refined. You see more silver and less pewter, more porcelain and less pottery, and a finer craftsmanship. Lace for curtains, silks in the damask patterns, pure linens for bedding, and usually more elegance.

French period pieces entered America first through New Orleans and then New York. The New Orleans French is more prevalent today. The French Provincial is more to our taste. The Country French is usually characterized by yellower wood such as the fruitwoods, magnolia, and pecan. The accessories have more curves than straight lines. The brass, copper, pewter and tin make excellent finishing touches. The fabrics are more typically plaids, toile de Jouy (French country scenes on a light ground), and rough textures in the French national colors of red, white, and blue with yellow added.

Colored lacquers have also played an important role, imitating the gold-leaf finishes of the wealthy by using a gold-color pigment (not metallic) or antique whites, blues, and reds.

Provincial French is gay, homey, and interesting. In accessories, it is close kin to Early American and Colonial. Many pieces now available are designed to be used in any of these periods. This is due to the versatility of today's designers, which makes our accessorizing easier.

The purer French furniture, such as Louis XV, is still used today in many apartments and homes. These are the delicately carved pieces with a Rococo feeling for bows, ribbons, shells, acanthus leaves, fruit, and flowers. This ornamentation can be found on the furniture, wall placques, mirror frames, and the like. The colors are pastel—the blues, golds, pinks and roses, soft greens, and ivories. The fabrics are

SPANISH-MEDITERRANEAN MOOD

always more delicate, including silks in damasks, brocades, velvets, voile, or taffeta weaves. The rugs are Savonnerie or Aubusson; the floors are usually wood parquet. Many mirrors, crystal chandeliers, and gold and bronze cast pieces are used. The furniture finishes are soft brown woods, white and gold lacquers, or pure gold leaf (today we use more gold metal leaf because of price). A present-day trend is also to have the lacquers in pastel colors, which can be very effective if properly done. The rooms that frame furniture should be spacious in feeling, with ceiling moulds and elaborate doors.

Mediterranean furniture can be Spanish or Italian or almost any other feeling that the manufacturer decides to mix in, such as Moorish designs and other touches. The pure Spanish or pure Mexican has its own charm, but requires great simplicity of living—much tile, hard floors, rough furniture bordering on the crude, handloomed fabrics, and darker pictures, often of a religious nature because of the great influence of the Catholic Church in both countries. White walls, beehive fireplaces, exposed-beamed ceilings, wrought-iron furniture, brightly colored accessories, and carved doors are the basic feeling. The rough fabrics are always gaily colored, almost gaudy, or else no color at all (off-white, which we call "gray goods").

The popular Italian today is really a more massive takeoff on the Traditional, but in a yellow wood rather than a browner mahogany. The accessories are more classic in feeling: obelisks, Roman busts, architectural features such as columns, friezes, and pedestals. Velvets, certain damask patterns and satins are more typically used in this colder, more formal atmosphere. The surfaces are hard and cold—marble, terrazo, ceramic tiles, stucco, and stone. Do not misconstrue this hardness as being without charm, since this type of home can be elegantly charming and mixes well with today's stark modern.

ITALIAN-CLASSIC MOOD

MODERN-CONTEMPORARY MOOD

I have always said that modern furniture is only for the very wealthy. My reasoning is this—as yet we have not established a definite trend in this design, and unlike the furniture of other periods, it has not stood the test of time. Consequently, you must have the means to continually update as the trends change. The key to modern decor is simplicity—utter and complete simplicity. The plastics, the stainless steel, and weathered woods and severity of styling require bold colors, considerable space, and a variety of textures either in walls, upholstery, or area rugs. The danger with modern furniture is a stark, sterile coldness. But do not confuse coldness with good modern decorating.

The abstract art that is so popular today is elusive. We have all read of the first prize taken by a child with paint on his feet walking over a canvas. This is the hazard not found in the realistic school. But who says a person cannot paint with his feet? My point is this: be sure you have an opinion or interpretation of your painting and that it gives you the feeling you want. This being the case, you should not care what others think. Life has enough limitations as it is without imposing additional ones upon yourself. After all, you are only as limited as you let yourself be. For many reasons, the modern interior is the coming trend. We are running out of hardwoods from which to manufacture furniture, and this has resulted in the use of glass, mirror, steel, and plastics. In our age of discovery, we will develop even more interesting and appealing textures for new designs, but never lose sight of the fact that what we have, regardless of period, is precious and should be maintained for posterity.

VI

MAINTAINING WHAT YOU OWN

IN MY LECTURES, I HAVE ALWAYS pointed out the necessity of knowing what you own or are about to purchase. Then there will be no problem in your mind as to what you can do with it and how you can care for it.

If it is wood, it should be properly washed every six months. This always leaves Mrs. Pace Setter aghast, but my comment is: "What would your windows look like if they were never washed!" There is a proper way to wash your furniture. Wash one part at a time, starting at the top. Use a bar of Ivory soap, a soft cloth and warm water. Wash the top well, rinse it well, and dry it well; then proceed to a side or a leg following the same process. Of course, soap or water left on a piece of wood any length of time would harm it, but I recommend washing, not soaking. A polish of light wax and diluted lemon oil, such as Guardsman, should then be applied. If it is a wood top that gets lots of use, a heavy paste floor wax is excellent. This heavy wax requires much elbow grease for a good polish.

The saddest thing that has happened to the furniture-polish industry is that almost 100 per cent of the aerosol-can polishes are mixed with a waterproofing agent which tends to close the pores of the wood. If you who amply apply it are a good housekeeper, such a polish will raise the finish. This coating prevents a fine finish from ever being applied again; and often the present finish assumes a cloudy grayish-white look. If you have ever seen the refinishing shop trying to remove this waterproofing agent with steel wool and pure bleach you would throw out every furniture polish in your pantry in an aerosol can. The trouble with advertising today is not so much what they tell you, but what they do not.

I dilute the Guardsman polish to keep it from being oily and attracting dust. This same polish is excellent for metals such as doorknobs, chandeliers, bathroom faucets, as well as hardware on furniture. Use Guardsman sparingly on the dustcloth, but give the item a healthy coat after each washing.

Upholstery cleaning has been made simple by a formula from one of the major chemical companies. Take one cup of hot water and enough Tide to make a foam, then add one cup of Energine Fireproof (ask your druggist for this item). Using a real sponge, not a plastic one, dip it in the solution and squeeze the water out of it. Then pick up some foam and go lightly over the soiled upholstery. This will damp-clean without saturation, thus leaving no ring. Your dirt went on in layers, and so it should be removed a layer at a time. A word of caution: Energine Fireproof is poisonous to some persons, either to breathe or to touch; therefore wear a mask and rubber gloves and ventilate well. If there is no grease or oil involved follow the same procedure, omitting the Energine Fireproof. This solution also works when spotting draperies or carpeting. My only other word of caution is: clean carefully and do not saturate. There are some people who can clean everything and others who cannot clean anything, so know your own limitations and proceed accordingly.

I am often asked whether one should have draperies cleaned. I favor not cleaning them too often. If you vacuum them regularly and they still smell dusty, it is time to clean. At the time you select your draperies, you should obtain an extra piece of fabric, have it cleaned to see if it shrinks, and find out whether it cleans best in a coin-operated machine or at a commercial cleaners. If it is washable, also remember to test a piece of your lining if lined and a piece of the crinoline if pleated. Save a piece of the original samples and measure before experimenting so you will have a guide for comparison. As a preliminary-planning precaution it is wise to pretest everything you purchase. These swatches are available at a small fee, and it is certainly a small price to pay for the knowledge gained. If you are told it's one of a kind and a special purchase with no fabric available, beware; there is something they are trying to hide from you. As in life you get exactly what you pay for and not a thing or a dollar is handed you on a silver platter. So stop kidding yourself and face reality.

For this reason I say pretest. Know what you are buying, how it will react under dirt, wear, and spills, how it can be cleaned, the texture it will have after cleaning, and you will be satisfied with the home furnishings you own.

Spots should be removed as soon as possible so that they do not have time to set. After spills, blot immediately, take a real sponge and cold water and try to remove the excess. Then use Tide and water foam.

The prisms on your chandeliers, the cut-glass pieces, and the crystal that are so lovely as accessories are best cleaned with very warm water and Cheer detergent. This idea was given me by a collector of cut glass, whose collection always sparkled no matter when I dropped in. Her formula lasts much longer than any other I have found.

Of course, being a Midwesterner by birth, I believe in kerosene in the window-washing water and a newspaper with which to polish them. No ready-mixed process has given me a more lasting sparkle.

I have stood at so many dirty front doors that at this point I would like to become an exterior designer and say scrub that front door as regularly as you dust the interior of your home. Keep this area fresh and clean since it is the first impression that is lasting. Greasy doorknobs, tarnished door knockers, greasy buttons on the doorbell, and dirty mailboxes are inexcusable. Much of what a client has to say loses its impact with this first impression because actions speak louder than words.

Many hard floors are being used in homes today, and there are many ways to seal them. If your floor is brick, d'Hanis, Saltillo tile, or some other hard porous surface, a formula of equal parts of boiled linseed oil and turpentine is excellent. Apply with a mop or rag, and remove all excess immediately. Let dry overnight, and when completely dry apply another coat and follow this process until you obtain the gloss you desire. Each additional coat adds more gloss. The secret is to let each coat of oil dry thoroughly, since with differences in humidity it is difficult to set a specific drying time. (Do not leave any excess on overnight.) This is also excellent on concrete or flagstone areas. Your fireplace brick or ledgestone can be enhanced in the same way. It is a sealer that only brings out the natural coloring in each tile, brick, or stone. After the floor is sealed you can dry or wet-mop it for a long period of time (from six months to a year). If only the traffic areas need a touch-up, this can be done without getting a patchy appearance. Slate must be treated differently. Clean with kerosene and wax if you desire a sheen.

For terrazzo, marble, or vinyl floors there are special sealers, and these should be applied professionally the first time.

Many clients have wrong conceptions of what terrazzo, marble, or tile should do. So again I say pretest for your family. Potato chips and other greasy foods can spot if such floors are not properly sealed and protected. The same applies to marble tops on furniture, since water rings and wine rings will show up if the marble is not properly waxed. These become permanent stains when liquids penetrate the pores, and there is no way to remove them.

With the shortage of woods, marbles, and slates, furniture designers are going to synthetics for substitutes. Most synthetics are more durable than natural materials, but they are not infallible. They do need cream waxes for protection, and they will burn if something hot is set upon them. Cigarettes will leave their mark if they slip off the ash tray. You can scratch them with a rough place on the bottom of an ash tray or planter. Buy some brown felt and Elmer's glue and get to work protecting your table tops.

I would be remiss if I did not remind you to use your Ivory soap and water process on the paneling in your home. And on your kitchen cabinets, too, if they are in a wood finish. Then after proper washing, use a paste paneling wax from your local grocer for the polishing. This will add life to your wood as well as a gleam you had forgotten it had.

Maintenance is constant hard work for which there are no short cuts, but lasting quality can be maintained and the budget remain free for added luxuries rather than for replacement. Continued maintenance is truly money in the bank.

VII

LIGHTING AND ACCESSORIES

THE BEST WAY TO CREATE MOODS in the home is by lighting. Dark, dreary rooms are being freed with windows cut in the walls, skylights added to ceilings, and solid walls replaced by glass to bring sunshine and daylight into our lives. This also requires properly placed artificial lighting so that the same effect can be created night or day.

My favorite lighting is the recessed low-voltage lights for spots of illumination on a plant, a painting, an interesting conversational grouping, to highlight a bar or a bookshelf, or to just indicate an entry. Well-placed mirrors can reflect the light to a remote, otherwise dark area.

I personally dislike fluorescent lighting in the home. If I use it at all, it is under the upper cabinets in a kitchen or butler's pantry. This eliminates the loss of too much space for light fixtures and serves as an excellent work area. Too many kitchens or work areas are not designed with the light reflecting on the project, but rather at one's back, and this casts a shadow. A word of caution about the color of lights used. A white daylight will not discolor the food and is a must in a food-preparation area. This also applies to the color selection of your tile or formica counters as well as the pottery or china on which you serve it. One of my most humorous memories is of a young couple, of whom the husband was an interior designer. Their pottery was a very fashionable ugly yellow-green, and their parties were always hilarious because of the incongruous food combinations they were forced to serve to look appetizing on these plates. Most of the red meats and green vegetables looked very sickly on them. From this experience, all of us learned an important lesson in color early in life, and today the husband is one of the more successful interior designers. My point is that color, especially in lighting, affects the surroundings. Therefore careful consideration must be given to the yellow in an incandescent bulb as well as the pink, blue, or green lights that are fashionable today. Some fluorescent bulbs remove color rather than add it, which can be even worse.

I insist on sufficient wattage to read, see, or study by. Reasonably priced rheostats (dimmers) are available today, so there is no excuse for insufficient light at any time.

Flush lights in the ceilings and fixtures covered with frosted covers are misused as Mr. or Mrs. Pace Setter place a large-wattage frosted bulb under this frosted shade. The result is double frosting, with at least half the wattage they are paying for lost within the fixture itself. A simple solution is a clear light bulb (one in which you can see the filament) in the wattage you need. Light bulbs of too high a wattage in an enclosed case get too hot and burn out quickly.

Bathroom and dressing-room lighting should be soft, but with enough wattage to meet the critical test of applying make-up or shaving. This is why sidelights or wall lights are better than overhead lights in this area. You should have a combination of the two if you require it.

Lighting in closets is a must no matter how shallow the closet, for the same reason as the kitchen cabinets: you want the light in front of you, not coming from behind.

With small, inconspicious lighting fixtures, there is no reason why most paintings or wall treatments cannot have a flush ceiling light spotted on them at low cost.

There is a new trend today in table lamps. Five years ago the base and shade had to be more or less equal; now the fashion is to have the base two-thirds the overall height and

the shade approximately one-third. This creates an illusion
of height and provides better illumination.

Our floor lamps are shorter, more slender, and much
neater in relation to the furniture among which they are
placed. I hope that torchieres and grotesque floor lamps will
be discarded in the future.

Chandeliers with tiny shades are beginning to be stylish
again. Both silk and crystal shades are used on the more
elaborate ones, with tiny metal shades on wood and metal
ones. The secret is the minute size. This effect throws the
light downward and upward, thus giving a more localized
light which accentuates the centerpeice and gives a soft light
to the room by reflecting on the ceiling. Again the rheostat
is used for a candlelight mood or the full effect of maximum
wattage.

Wall sconces, both electric ones and candles, give an interesting ornamentation to an otherwise drab area. The electric ones especially are most effective with miniature shades.
I like to burn candles, with protective glass shades, for lighting effect. The main caution is to place these away from air
conditioning vents, so that the candles burn slowly. Candles
are a must at parties because they eliminate the accumulation
of cigarette smoke. Being highly allergic to smoke, I burn
candles nightly. Whenever I help a friend or client plan a
party I give consideration to the candles first.

If you have glass walls consider the lighting directly
outside the glass area. Strategically placed lights create an
interesting play of design on the night shadows. A lighted
fountain seen from inside a home is most relaxing, as is a
lighted aquarium on the interior.

Today's homes reflect the indoor-outdoor look our architects have developed under the influence of Frank Lloyd
Wright. Therefore, more live plants are planned in interiors,
and these require a special lighting to accent them. An electric

light left burning over a plant will cause it to grow steadily with little or no natural light. Light also brings out a plant's beauty, so it serves a twofold purpose.

When planning your electrical layout, plan the intercom system with a stereo hookup. My most frequent complaint to the electrician is that he strings out the light switches, the intercom, and thermostats so that several walls are rendered useless for hanging pictures, placques, or planters. It is far more convenient to make a cluster of these switches.

While on the electrical system, I must say that I cannot understand the electricians and painters who will tell you not to paint the plastic switch plates and base plugs. This is nonsense. Semi-gloss paint stays on and washes beautifully. So beware when they advise against painting. The painter is trying to take a short cut, and the electrician does not want to bring the plates ahead of time.

The more subtle the background, the more interesting the furniture and accessory arrangement of your home. Play up the simplicity, which is never easy, and then more accessories can be used.

Accessorizing a home is the art of selecting accessories, and it is a major one, for it reflects the true image of the person or persons occupying a home. The right light must shine on the right accessory. Do not have anything on your walls or furniture you do not like. Each accessory you display presents a part of your real personality. So if you are displaying something in your home you do not like, you are lying to yourself, your family, your friends, and to the visitor that comes to your door.

At this point, I must remind you that these accessories are the jewelry of your room. Of course, we would all like to have priceless jewels, but many of us cannot afford them. We have however, found suitable substitutes we can afford that enhance an ensemble we own. We can do the same with our home furnishings. Use great care in selecting the lamps, the ash trays, the vases, the pieces of sculpture, and the wall hangings that mean something to you, the individual.

I am opposed to smoking, but this does not keep my family and friends from doing it; therefore, I provide large well-designed ash trays for them. They educated me long ago to the fact that small trays only invite burns on my table tops. These do not have to be ugly to be practical.

The boldness of size is a must with planters. My only disclaimer is that they must not overlap the sides of their table or stand. The greenery can, perhaps, but not the pot. This also applies to lampshades. You need to view each room with the trained eye of your interior designer, who understands the proper proportions of scale and balance.

I select lamps and accessories for clients, but we (the client and I) spend much time over the selection of pictures and paintings for the walls. It is necessary that the client's feelings should be reflected in these accessories. I spend much time observing my clients to see where their interests lie, so that I can offer them alternatives as the job reaches completion. Even in the early planning stages, I begin to explore their thoughts on this subject, because we often do not know where our interests lie if we have never previously examined them. A person may have had his life touched by a tragedy at sunset, and as a result a sunset seascape or landscape would not appeal to him. Someone may have had a very humble beginning and an unhappy youth which makes him object to shacks or dilapidated buildings in a landscape. I have a painting hanging in my living room with a very prominent shack about which I was questioned at the time of purchase. I enjoy it as much as I do rural scenes and seascapes, but do not want to influence a client's thinking because of a personal preference. If it is obvious I have decorated a home, then I have failed. Interior designers are taught that we must interpret the client's wants, needs, likes, and dislikes, not our own.

Contemporary artists fall into several stylistic categories. Let's begin with the abstract, which is an unusual impression of an artist's idea and creates different emotions in each individual viewer. To me this is what makes abstracts interesting. They have unusual coloring, whether extremely subtle or overpoweringly harsh.

The realistic school is extremely easy—as "a rose is a rose is a rose." I like things to look as they are in some instances, and this type of art is especially easy to understand. It may be to your advantage to find which artists are now making a name for themselves so as to make the best investment possible when you are spending your money on realism.

Impressionistic art is steadily gaining in popularity and has been since the time of Monet and Renoir. The contemporary artists who paint in this style are extremely talented, and this art is very popular. The impressionist school is a compromise between abstraction and realism.

I personally like good watercolors or etchings along with my oil paintings. These are both a finer kinds of work. The techniques are more subtle and require a more critical eye.

I am not ignoring collages and other art forms, but space limitations preclude consideration of them all. By merely mentioning them I hope to whet your appetite, so that you will ask your favorite designer to help you develop these interests.

Cherished old pieces should be proudly displayed and protected. This is why peer cabinets are so popular today. They give us a chance to display our treasures and protect them at the same time. Many collectors and hobby enthusiasts have a problem in that they tend to overcollect or overwork their hobby. The person who does needlepoint well will have some in every room. My advice to this kind of person is to make herself a piece or two and plan to give the rest away. The mass production or bargain-basement look certainly detracts from the beauty of the individual pieces. This is not confined to only one hobby, but includes them all—ceramics, metalwork, knitting, woodwork, embroidery, and collecting, whether cups and saucers, cut glass, bottles, silver, or hand-painted china.

Probably one of the most interesting ideas to come out of decorating today is the display of various shapes and sizes of wall decor grouped over a piece of furniture such as a credenza, sofa, or some other large piece. This can be a most effective way to exhibit your treasures. Scale and balance are the only prerequisites for a grouping of this sort, and it must be balanced with the other walls and accessories in the room. Of course, it must not be over a very busily patterned sofa since the pattern formed by the wall decor will conflict with that of the sofa. This is the perfect place for the tiny "eyeball" we spoke of earlier to add a soft mood light to the area.

Candelabra, sconces, or single candlesticks are always effective accessories in any area from the kitchen to the bathroom and all the rooms in between. These can be made of metal, wood, ceramic, plaster of Paris, depending on your particular decor.

Books, old or new, are always effective. Figurines of any description and material are interesting accents. The only prerequisite is that you personally like them—do not just use them as fillers.

Many bibelots do not necessarily fall within the realm of a normal accessory; but as long as they have meaning for you, find a way to display them. An old fan in a frame, a pocket watch in a glass dome, some antique buttons of an unusual quality framed as a picture, a collection of old jewelry with a removable back so that you can sometimes wear the pieces and display them at other times, Grandfather's sword hung on the wall, Grandmother's wicker basket or copper kettle filled with flowers or greenery—you are your only limitation. Just go to your attic or storeroom, look and think.

One of the most unusual homespun ideas I have seen recently was an old washboard gayly colored with cork board replacing the ridged area and hung as a bulletin board. People are quite clever. I point this out because it is often such a simple thing properly done that creates beauty.

We cannot ignore the bathrooms when accessorizing. These rooms have become increasingly glamorous, and today many millions are spent on various plumbing fixtures alone. The faucets have become pieces of jewelry in solid brass, silver or gold plated, and in the most intricate designs from dolphins and swans' heads to starfish and flowers. I will hang an original oil painting or etching or well-framed group of watercolors in any bath today. Colorful flowers or greenery arrangements help to soften the effect. Seventy-five percent of the better homes have carpeting in the baths. Just consider first and foremost that the water and steam are prevalent in these areas so select the accessories with this in mind.

Remember that our water for bathing and drinking today has many chemicals that affect the metals and the hard surfaces, therefore, extreme caution should be exercised in their selection.

Likewise our kitchens are being glamorized into decorative areas, not only for cooking, but for enjoying too. We accessorize these areas with decorative tiles, colorful counter tops, wallpaper, and a surprise of bright colors on the interior of the cabinets. Today unique cannisters are being designed, gay dish towels are available, and the racks for cooking pots really should be seen. As a cook, I welcome all the wonderful improvements which make cooking more convenient down to the practical and decorative spice racks. There are interior designers today who specialize exclusively in kitchens.

Accessories portray you and your family who live in your home. So tell it like it is.

Many people's tastes are much more sophisticated than others. Just be especially careful that you interpret your own taste and your own ideas in your home, no matter how simple, rather than the ideas of friends, family, or your interior designer.

Those people with the simplest tastes are the best educated, emotionally balanced, and socially admired of all the people of the land. It is the overpowering, unsure middle class or nouveaux riches who at times try to impose their poor, immature taste in design on the people who really are and want to remain simple. Simplicity is elegance.

Our world is made of many cultures. Some we understand while many others are quite foreign to our way of life. Our lack of understanding does not make them wrong, but in our society only well-educated people seem to appreciate them.

We so want to be acceptable to our society today, and this controls much of our behavior. As I see the many tense faces on the streets I want to say "Stay loose, relax, be yourself and be happy." This is one of the many things we must teach our children. I am always a little sad when I hear that a couple who speak a foreign tongue teach only English to their children.

We are people of the world today and must think and act in this manner. The parents must teach their children to understand this and the finer things of life. If you do not teach those who share your roof how to use your silver, china, crystal and finer linens, where are they going to learn? Too many of us put such accessories away, and they are never seen by the younger members of the family. This also applies to exposure to fine art.

The cost of an afternoon at the museum is negligible compared to any other form of recreation but no one person could individually afford the price of the information and the beauty received. Through this exposure you will learn and teach your family the difference between fine and poor art. This won't occur in one trip or five, but eventually they will learn the difference.

Why all of this in an interior-design book? The best part of living in any home is to create and build an image of your own individual culture. This is you, your heritage, and it is wonderful no matter what it is. This is you, the real you, so reflect it in your home. If you think people are dull, look within because that's where the dullness lies. Use a little self-analysis, and find those exciting dreams and desires that you have always wanted to express. As I said earlier in the book—dare to be different. Understand your family's needs as well as your own, relax and express them.

We as individuals should live and respect each other. We have chocolate ice cream because everyone doesn't like vanilla. The same holds true with our home furnishings. We all enjoy different interests, different activities and recreations. Let your home as well as your life reflect your individuality. Be yourself, but understand the other cultures.

VIII

FIRE AND STORM DAMAGE

IN MY PROFESSION I HAVE ASSISTED with many insurance claims over the past twenty years. There are certain things you need to do at the beginning to save all you can of your possessions, and there are many damages that will not show up immediately after such a tragedy. My first advice is to check immediately on your insurance policy, and ask the agent what it will and will not cover. Too many people are not properly insured. Their thinking is, "It will never happen to me!" I would like to ask them, "If it does happen to you, can you come out of it satisfactorily with your present insurance?"

If it is a case of fire in only one room, be sure to check for smoke damage throughout the entire house. Usually many areas, if not all, are affected by the smoke. It will discolor the draperies, carpets, and upholstery in rooms behind closed doors. If a piece of upholstered furniture was soaked with water or filled with smoke, you must strip it down to the frame. Reglue the frame, repaint the springs, and replace all the stuffing in order to deodorize it. Dry these pieces of furniture as soon as possible in a shady place away from direct sunlight. Don't be surprised if the price of reupholstering is more than the original purchase price. This is an individual job with as much and frequently more work than was originally required in the factory.

If your rugs are soaked they will usually shrink. Area rugs not burned or otherwise stained can probably be cleaned and reused. But if they are damaged in any way, insist on their being restored to your satisfaction, otherwise replace them.

Usually your draperies shrink from hanging while wet. However, stains from dirty water are almost never removed by cleaning. In estimating a replacement, take into consideration the higher prices today over the price you paid when you bought them.

Mildew is a big factor in any of these claims. Since it is a mold, it does destroy. Check carefully for it under your various upholstered pieces, between carpet, pad, and floor, and behind pictures. A mildew retardant such as Lysol will discourage it.

All of your wooden pieces should be surface-dried immediately and put in the shade to dry thoroughly. If you have electricity turn a fan directly on them. After they are thoroughly dried give them an Ivory soap bath, and apply a generous coat of Guardsman polish or lemon oil to revitalize the wood as described in Chapter VI.

Always plan to reupholster and restore your home furnishings because there is depreciation on replacement, and your pieces are of a better quality than a replacement purchased today.

The insurance companies have a tremendous depreciation scale in most instances. Of course, it is generally known that the adjustor receives a percentage of the saving to the company in many cases, so it is to your advantage to have accurate figures on these repairs. Remember the adjustor is working for the insurance company, not for you.

Make a complete inventory of possessions in the affected area and have a careful examination of each item made by a professional. Today a standard fee for such an estimate is $25.00. Include everything affected, and scrutinize it for any possible damage.

As to the structure, most sheetrock is useless once it is

saturated, as is all insulation. Do not be hasty in settling your claims, since things continue to show up from a week to two months later. Tear into the walls that may have burned or been damaged by storm and are now filled with water, and dry them out thoroughly. Look for water stains or smoke damage on your wallpaper or painted walls, usually near the ceiling on seemingly undamaged walls. Remember smoke fumes can also cause damage.

Rising water is rarely covered by insurance, so it is most important to stack you furniture if you see this happening. Tie up your draperies, put pots and pans under your furniture legs, and if a considerable rise in water is expected choose your less valuable pieces and stack the others on top of them.

When these tragedies occur we are never thinking clearly. Get organized immediately afterwards, and get as much done as soon as possible. Too often people let things that could be saved get ruined.

Start today and inventory your possessions; take snapshots and put them in a strongbox, so there will be a written description and estimate of their value, plus a visual record of your precious pieces. This inventory will prove to be invaluable when included with a will. Update your records today.

IX

FEES AND A. I. D.

SO OFTEN WE WOULD LIKE to be someone other than we are. Either through want of training or capability we sometimes lack the know-how to do certain things. These are commonly known as shortcomings, and every human being has them; but because we seem to have talents that may lie in an unglamorous field we try to become something we are not and never will be. This is so often the birth of an interior-decorator homemaker, who uses the excuse "I want the home to look like me and my family and not like some interior designer!" Much too late we professionals inherit these clients who expect us to wave a magic wand and eliminate their errors without additional cost. This is pure ignorance on the part of the homemaker.

The interior-designing profession is a most important field, and it has come of age within my own lifetime. Really intelligent people have an interior designer who can advise them. Designers realize the need of thrift in making home-furnishing purchases, and thrift, mind you, does not mean cheap; it means care and understanding in purchasing.

In 1931 the American Institute of Decorators was formed, and over the past forty years it has grown into a group of professionals who are in great demand the world over. These people have designed some of the most beautiful interiors in the world.

"The Interior Designer is a person qualified, by training and experience, to plan and supervise the design and execution of interiors and their furnishings and to organize the various arts and crafts essential to their completion."*

Isn't it a wonderful thought to know these people (over 4,500 strong) are available to you for your home? Like all professionals, designers charge a fee for their services, but it is not beyond the reach of the average citizen of this country.

There are many initials following the names of various groups of designers, but none are even one-third the age or demand the high qualifications required by the A.I.D., which now stands for the American Institute of Interior Designers. Why the change of name? Because of the growth of the profession and the fact that training began to go beyond the realm of just hanging draperies, placing furniture, and the like. We really design interiors.

This, of course, did not just happen. The educational horizon for this profession has broadened immeasurably, and experience has taught us about people. More emphasis has been placed on environmental behavior, and we are constantly learning that certain character traits are revealed when we use certain colors or certain periods of furniture. We are a walking map of what we are and what we have made of ourselves. We dress the way we do because we want to, we live the way we do for the same reason.

Often unknown to ourselves, we do not portray ourselves as we want to be seen because of our lack of education in good design, scale and balance, and fine art.

This is the point at which your interior designer becomes a real help to you. Someone who through conversation can piece together the real you, this designer learns of your needs, your wants, your desires for your own way of living, and puts together an image that is you.

---

*Definition officially approved by American Institute of Interior Designers.

This is not done with a magic wand. It is done through experience and training for this purpose—to make a better place for an individual to live. As I said earlier, and it bears repeating, "If you can tell I have professionally decorated a home, then I as a designer have failed." My identity is supposed to be unknown. It is the identity of the family occupying the home that is to be visible to the eye. Working this closely together, personalities must be compatible, and care must be exercised in selecting your designer.

Check her work and see if basically you like what you see. Inquire of the designer and her temperament. If she is a personality you can work with, then consult her.

It is most important to lay your cards on the table. Discuss the work you want done and the amount of money you wish to spend, so that the designer can get the most out of the money you have to invest.

Today the interior designer requires no license to operate; this does not, therefore, preclude anyone from labeling herself an interior decorator or designer. So you must look for the initials after the name to be sure that yours is the person with the experience and education best qualified to assist you.

Anyone who is qualified to be a member of A.I.D. will be one. Many have to settle for a lesser title. A.I.D. does not reject anyone who is qualified.

It is always reassuring to have an advisor you can depend on to tell you to take the paper or covering off your lampshades or not to display candles until the wick is burned; that there are drapes on dresses, but on the windows they are draperies; that mauve is pronounced "mō-ve" not "maw-ve"; and the myriad other things too numerous to mention.

At this point I would like to point out, in behalf of all interior designers, that because of their closeness to you, the client, you have a tendency to impose upon them, whether paid or not, because they do understand you. Be considerate of these professionals, and do not expect them to attend every social event on your home-entertainment calendar.

The professional expects to be compensated for her time at the rate of from $10 to $50 or more per hour, depending on the individual or firm. This charge can be paid by fees or commissions on goods purchased. There is a simple way to find out what your interior designer will charge—just ask.

This is indeed money in the bank throughout the years because of the beauty of your rooms, the proper functioning of space, and the durability of the furnishings therein—all the result of profession services rendered.

Because of interior designers, chemical companies, environmental institutes, and the design world in general, which are looking to your needs as an individual and as a family, you can become a more complete person.

In our lifetime we have seen and will continue to see more progress in every field than any generation before us. We live well and enjoy many of the luxurious comforts that were once limited to the wealthy few. Call your interior designer today and get to work on that project you have been delaying.

See the beauty around you, the beauty that radiates from within for each of us. Show the world what you and your family are. Live and let live in peace with each other. Create beauty wherever and whenever you can. Each small effort shows as the many grains of sand makes a dune. Now as you close this book look about you with fresh eyes. Do you like what you see? If not, start changing it now.